Written by Mary-Anne Creasy

Illustrated by Ian Forss

Flying Start
to Literacy®

A note from the author

When I go to the beach with my family, we leave very early in the morning, so often we arrive when the sun is still rising. Early morning is the best time for surfing, as the wind is often coming from the beach, so the waves are slow and smooth. There are a lot of kids who surf there, some are about 10 or 12 years old. They live near the beach, ride their bikes there early, have a quick surf, then go to school.

These kids were the inspiration for this story. Watching them from the beach, I do see the occasional wipe-out, and it's easy to imagine what could happen.

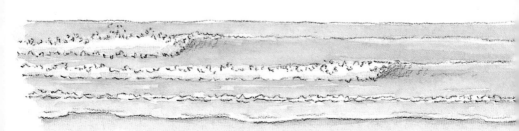

Contents

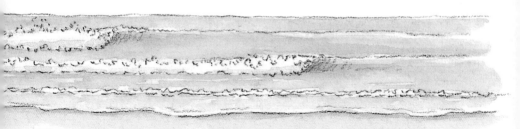

Chapter 1
The day before

Tom got up early and put on his wetsuit. He grabbed his surfboard and rode his bike down to the beach, his board gripped under his arm.

It was overcast and drizzling lightly. The weather report on the radio said that there would be perfect waves. The surf would be just right. Tom dropped his bike on the grass and walked down to the sand.

Trucks had started arriving, full of gear for the weekend's surf competition. Tom had signed up for the under-13 section, and his mum had paid the entry fee. Even though it was quite a lot of money, his mum said she didn't mind paying because she knew how much Tom loved surfing and wanted to compete.

But that seemed so long ago now. He closed his eyes and tried to remember the feelings of excitement and confidence he had back then – only last week.

Tom strapped the leg-rope of his board onto his ankle and carried the board to the water's edge. The waves were rolling in. He watched the surf crashing down. As the water surged over his feet, his heart began to pound. He suddenly began to gasp for breath and he squeezed his eyes shut as he tried to block the memory, but the feeling of drowning flooded all his senses.

Tom went back to the sand and sat down,
watching the surf. An hour in the surf
would have been a perfect way to spend
some time before school. He had done
the same thing nearly every day for the past
two years. But he hadn't even stepped into
the water since that day – that day last
week when he nearly drowned.

Chapter 2
Wipe-out!

It had only been one week since it happened.
It had been a sunny day on the weekend.
Tom had slept in, so by the time he got to
the beach, it was crowded and there was a
long line of surfers bobbing up and down on
the waves.

Tom didn't like to surf when it was crowded,
and he almost went home, but he knew he
had to practise before the competition. He
still didn't have his cutback just right, where
he had to turn in toward the wave while he
was surfing and then surf out.

Tom jumped on his board and paddled far out, away from the families and the beginner surfers. He straddled his board and waited for a wave.

The surf had been a bit flat where he was, but he knew the waves would soon pick up. And, sure enough, before long he felt the swell rise beneath him and drop gently down.

"Here it comes," he said out loud.

Tom saw a wave beginning to form. It looked good. He started to paddle toward the shore, keeping an eye on the wave.

The wave rose up behind him, until it looked like a huge blue mountain. He paddled faster to beat the crest. He stood up quickly and began to ride the wave.

It was big. The top of the wave towered over him and pushed him downward. He shuffled further back so the front of the board stayed up. He crouched down and turned the board to practise his cutback move.

But the wave was too fast. His board
went straight into the face of the wave and
flipped him over. He was dragged
down into the churning water, spinning
round and round.

Tom's board was being sucked down. He tried to reach his leg-rope to rip it off, but he couldn't bend his leg as the force of the water was pulling him down. Finally, he managed to rip the leg-rope off and free himself from his board. He tried to find the sandy bottom of the ocean to push himself up. He kicked out, hoping to feel the sand. But he didn't know which way was up!

Tom's lungs were bursting, his heart was pounding, and his nose and throat were stinging from the seawater. It seemed to get darker. He wanted to scream for help. He could feel his body becoming weaker.

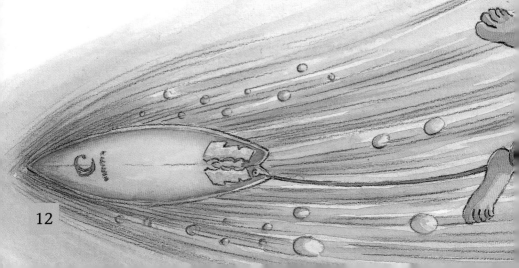

Suddenly Tom felt the sand beneath his feet. With his last bit of strength, he pushed down and his head burst out into the sunshine. He gasped and tilted his head back and breathed in and out quickly, filling his lungs with air before another wave came.

He ploughed through the surf, staggered onto the beach and fell down on the sand, looking up at the sky. He was still gasping for air. He concentrated on breathing calmly – in through his nose and out through his mouth, until the dizzy feeling stopped.

Chapter 3
No more surf

After a few minutes, Tom got up and found his board washed onto the beach. A lifeguard was standing near it, looking annoyed.

"Hey you, that board nearly cracked a kid's head open. Keep your leg-rope on next time," he said crossly.

Tom looked at him and went to his board. He staggered slightly and fell on the sand.

"You okay?" the lifeguard asked. He bent down to look at Tom.

Tom squeezed his eyes shut and nodded. Tears were forming. He picked up his board, tucked it under his arm and rode home.

All around him, everything was so normal. People were laughing and eating, playing and swimming. No one looked at him.

Tom had nearly drowned and no one had noticed.

Not only that, his mum was annoyed when he got home.

"I told you to mow the lawn before you went surfing, Tom."

Tom just looked at her. He almost said it – I nearly drowned, Mum.

But then he remembered her warnings, her worry and how she was always reminding him about the danger of drowning out in the rough surf. If he said anything, that would be it. No more surfing.

Chapter 4
Drop out!

Now here Tom was, the day before the competition. And he hadn't been back in the water since. He would have to drop out. He would have to make up an excuse not to do it.

He rode home just as his mum was making breakfast. He stripped off his wetsuit and hung it up.

"What's up? Surf no good today?" she asked.

Tom felt his hair. He'd forgotten to wet it before he left the beach. He'd been doing that for the past week so she would think everything was normal.

"Um, yeah," he mumbled, and quickly left the room to get ready for school.

When Tom got home after school, his mum was looking happy.

"I've got the day off tomorrow, so I can watch you surf," she said. "We can go out for breakfast and make a great day of it."

"Oh, great," said Tom. He knew how hard it was for his mum to get Saturdays off. She worked at the surf club and Saturday was a busy day.

Chapter 5
Into the surf?

In the morning, Tom stayed in bed, listening to his mum getting ready, humming to the radio. He began to moan quietly, but she didn't hear. He moaned louder and clutched his stomach. His mum stuck her head around the doorway.

"Are you getting up? I've got a table booked for breakfast at eight o'clock."

"I don't feel well," said Tom, as he turned and moaned again.

"Are you a bit nervous?" asked his mum. "That's normal. It's good to be a bit nervous."

She opened the curtains on the windows and the sunshine streamed in.

"But Mum, I don't feel good." Tom shut his eyes and turned to the wall.

"Don't be silly. Come on, I'm ready."

Tom felt his heart pounding. He would have to tell her.

"Mum," Tom said quietly.

"Yes?" she said, as she came back into his room.

"Mum?" Tom's voice shook a little.

"Tom, what is it?" she asked, as she put her arms around him and hugged him.

"Mum, I can't go in the competition today." He couldn't look at her when he spoke.

"Why not? What's happened?" she asked.

Tom looked down at his hands. "The other day, last weekend, I went out in the surf. I had a bad surf. I ..." He couldn't finish.

"Oh, Tom, you'll be okay. You're not a bad surfer. You're great. You'll do fine."

She laughed and ruffled his hair.

He tried again.

"No, Mum. You don't understand. I nearly drowned."

She looked at him, but said nothing. She knelt back down and hugged him. She was silent for a few moments.

"It's okay, Tom," she said. "You didn't drown, did you? You're here, in bed, and it's a beautiful day. You don't have to go in the surf competition if you don't want to."

Tom thought about what his mum had said. She was right – he didn't have to do it. But he could go down to the beach and watch the competition. He suddenly felt better.

When Tom and his mum got to the beach, it was crowded with spectators and surfers. Sirens were wailing and people were shouting and whistling at the surfers.

It's so exciting. Maybe I can do it, thought Tom. One bad experience can't stop me from ever surfing again!

Tom signed in and drew out a number. He was in the first heat. He put his leg-rope on, took a deep breath and walked towards the surf.